Up to the Plate

The
All American Girls
Professional
Baseball League

by Margot Fortunato Galt

Lerner Publications Company • Minneapolis

To my husband Fran, who took me out to the ball game for the first time and remains my expert of last resort in matters of major-league baseball history and statistics.

Library of Congress Cataloging-in-Publication Data

Galt, Margot Fortunato.
   Up to the plate: the All American Girls Professional Baseball
League / by Margot Fortunato Galt.
      p. cm.
   Includes index.
   ISBN 0-8225-3326-X
   1. All-American Girls Professional Baseball League–History–Juvenile
literature. [1. All-American Girls Professional Baseball League–History.
2. Baseball–History.] I. Title.
GV875.A56G35 1995
796.357'64'0973–dc20   94-10636

Manufactured in the United States of America

1 2 3 4 5 6 – I/JR – 00 99 98 97 96 95

Contents

Rosie the Riveter on a Pitcher's Mound

On a cold, blustery, April afternoon in 1943, the phone rang at 17-year-old Sophie Kurys's home in Flint, Michigan. On the line were two friends from Sophie's fast-pitch softball team. Their voices were hurried and excited. They were coming to pick her up: Johnny Gottselig, a famous hockey player from Chicago, was in town to recruit young women for a new ball league. Sophie looked out the window: snow flurries. "He won't have tryouts in this weather," she retorted. "Anyway, I'm wearing a sweater and skirt."

Her friends insisted. Gottselig was holding tryouts in the high school gymnasium, where the windows were screened—she could hit the ball as hard as she liked. Reluctantly Sophie went along.

Once at the gym, Sophie hit and caught grounders off the floor. As always, she played intensely and hard. Her two friends didn't make the team, but Gottselig gave Sophie a ticket to Chicago for the next round of tryouts.

Opposite page: Sophie Kurys was recruited in 1943 and played with the league for nine years.

With millions of men in the armed forces during World War II, women were needed to staff assembly lines and manufacturing plants.

By April 1943, the United States had been fighting in World War II for more than a year. Thousands of men had been recruited and shipped overseas to bases and battlefields in Europe and the Pacific. The war was also about to send Sophie Kurys, along with 100 other young women from 17 states and Canada, away from home to try out for jobs they had never dreamed possible.

Like the famous character Rosie the Riveter, who quickly learned to rivet airplanes together when the men went overseas to fight, the ball-playing girls were on the move. They were leaving traditional roles for women and seizing an opportunity created by the demands of the war. Rather than a welding torch or a riveter, they would use a soft-ball bat and a glove. Instead of working in a factory, they'd work on a baseball field.

The American home front was focused on the war. Gas, meat, shoes, and sugar were rationed because these things were needed overseas. Trains were too busy carrying soldiers and war materials to transport meat and potatoes for civilians. Few people bought new cars because General Motors, Ford, Chrysler, and Nash now made airplanes and tanks instead.

Brides followed their husbands to military camps in distant states, and men whose poor eyesight, flat feet, or age kept them from military duty took jobs in faraway defense plants. Jobs were plentiful, and small towns in the Midwest jumped in population almost overnight when thousands of workers arrived to make airplane engines or synthetic rubber.

Rosie the Riveter inspired American women to take on new challenges during the war years.

Joe DiMaggio (left) joins the U.S. Army.

President Franklin Delano Roosevelt knew that the people at home were working harder than ever. They were making do with rationed food, clothing, and gasoline and were worried about their loved ones fighting overseas. Roosevelt believed the American people needed a regular, inexpensive, and familiar sport to entertain them and take their minds off the war. He supported baseball.

But baseball commissioner Judge Kenesaw Mountain Landis had actually considered canceling the 1942 major-league season. Baseball greats like Joe DiMaggio were being shipped overseas. Not only were many players leaving for the armed forces, some newspaper sportswriters wondered if, in good conscience, "husky hurlers" should continue to play the sport while spectacled clerks, salesmen, and fathers stormed enemy beaches.

The president wanted no baseball player to shirk his military duty, but he called on Landis and baseball club owners to keep the sport alive. Roosevelt thought that civilians working "longer hours and harder than ever before...ought to have a chance for recreation." He argued, "Even if the actual quality of the teams is lowered by the greater use of older players, this will not dampen the popularity of the sport."

Neither President Roosevelt (above left) nor Philip K. Wrigley (above) wanted baseball to die out during the war.

Enter Chicago Cubs owner Philip K. Wrigley of the chewing gum empire. In the fall of 1942, Wrigley gathered together a team of baseball professionals to help him devise a way to compensate for the loss of major-league manpower. The advisers suggested starting a women's baseball league. If women could stand in on assembly lines, they could surely pitch, bunt, and steal bases on vacant diamonds.

With teams like the Chicks, Chicago had a tradition of "powder-puff" ball. Across the nation and in Canada, some 40,000 semipro women's softball teams drew enthusiastic hometown crowds. They were sponsored, as *Time* magazine reported in April 1943, by "breweries, taverns, bakeries, big industries, and little individuals with a yen to see their names scrawled across the satin backs or sweatered fronts of cavorting U.S. tomboys."

Why couldn't Wrigley send the scouts of the Chicago Cubs coast-to-coast to discover female hurlers and sluggers to make up a new women's ball league? He could and he did.

Wrigley and his team of advisers selected a no-nonsense name to emphasize the new league's patriotic origin: the All American Girls Professional Baseball League. The name was also intended to distinguish the league from "undignified" women's softball teams, with names like Slapsie Maxie's Curvaceous Cuties or the Num Num Pretzel Girls. The new league, Wrigley insisted, would be made up of "moral, feminine" players.

Selecting from a number of small towns where men's softball or baseball leagues were popular, Wrigley and his advisers decided to base teams in four midwestern cities: Racine, Wisconsin; Kenosha, Wisconsin; South Bend, Indiana; and Rockford, Illinois. From its very outset, the game would be different than softball.

Softball, played with a large ball—12 inches around—was a pitcher's game. The fast, "windmill" style of pitching was exciting to watch, with some pitchers whipping their arms round and round in a dizzying fashion, bamboozling poor batters by letting go of the ball while their arms were still turning. But even such dazzling deliveries couldn't speed a softball as fast as a baseball, and batters couldn't hit the big ball as fast or far.

Furthermore, in softball, the distances between the pitcher's mound and home plate, and between the bases, were so short that leading off, stealing, and sliding were not allowed (because runners could too easily beat the big, wind-resistant ball). Traditionally only the catcher and first baseman wore gloves.

Wrigley and his advisers pondered how to keep the equipment of softball, familiar to most female ballplayers, yet liven up the game's hitting, running, and fielding. They resorted to a compromise. The new game would use nine-player teams, instead of softball's ten. All the distances on the field—from home plate to mound, mound to first

Wrigley expected fans to be drawn to ballparks by the novelty of women playing what was considered a man's sport.

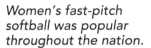

**Rosie the Riveter
on a Pitcher's
Mound**

*Women's fast-pitch
softball was popular
throughout the nation.*

base, and base to base—would be expanded. All players in the new league would use gloves, thus encouraging harder throws. Leading off, stealing, and sliding would be allowed, but the league would retain the wind-up, underhand pitching style of fast-pitch softball. With the rules decided, all Wrigley had to do was choose the players.

——————Big-League Salaries ——————

When Sophie Kurys arrived in Chicago, it was raining. The big city was noisy and bustling. She knew none of the 100 other young women invited to Wrigley Field to try out for the new league.

Since childhood, Kurys had been knocking the stuffing out of a softball, then rewrapping it with butcher's string. On a lot kitty-corner from her house, she played with her friend Squirt and other boys. Every morning, she couldn't wait to get outside and play. Baseball and softball were the best parts of her life.

Up to the Plate

Kay Heim came down from Canada for an opportunity to play professional ball.

Now, in the big, unfamiliar city, surrounded by strangers, she was homesick and unhappy. "What am I doing here?" she asked herself. "I can play ball at home." But once out on Wrigley Field (home field for the Chicago Cubs), she began to relax with the other prospective players.

As they warmed up, played three-inning games, and jogged around the ballpark, Sophie and the rest of the young women measured their chances of being selected against the abilities of the other prospects—the best female ballplayers in the country. They knew they were fast and could get on base. They could pitch hard and accurately, bunt and hit too. Though awed by the skill of their competitors, the women told themselves they'd make the league.

After a few days, Philip Wrigley and his advisers met to select the four teams. Instead of each player being signed by a team as in men's baseball, the women in the All American Girls League were under contract to the league as a whole. Then, on the basis of "the division of player wealth," each team was staffed to balance all the others. No single team was supposed to have more talent than any other.

Whittling down the 100 hopefuls to 60 or so—15 on each team—Wrigley and his advisers were ready to deliver the news to the players. On the day of the announcement, managers and trainers told the women that two large chalkboards would face them as they came down the stairs into the Cubs' dressing room. If a woman found her name on one of the boards, she would be, for the next five months, a Racine Belle, a Kenosha Comet, a South Bend Blue Sox, or a Rockford Peach. Nervous but confident, Sophie Kurys descended the stairs and found her name scrawled under the heading "Racine Belles." Her manager would be Johnny Gottselig, the man who had recruited her to try out for the league.

Kay Heim, a catcher from Edmonton, Canada, had received her summons to Chicago late. While the other young women were working out in Wrigley Field, she was still contemplating the long train ride from Edmonton. Heim had started playing on a city baseball team called the Edmonton Eskimos when she was 12. She was 22 and bookkeeping for the fancy McDonald Hotel when she received a letter inviting her to tryouts in Chicago. By then she had moved to a fast-pitch softball team called Orange Crush, and from there to the fast-pitch Edmonton Pats. She was the pride of local newspapers, which called her "one of the [area's] best all-around performers...and one of the leading hitters."

One of 13 Canadians recruited for the league in 1943, Heim arrived in Chicago a few days after spring training. When she reported to Wrigley's office, she was sent immediately to join the Kenosha Comets, playing in Racine. After a short train trip, Kay went directly to Horlick Field, where the Comets and the Belles were having morning practice.

The promise of good money was as much a lure to the league as the chance to play professional, new-style ball.

She was given a uniform on the spot. "Get out there and play," the manager told her. "I could tell every girl was watching me closely," she remembered. The next day Kay was installed as a regular catcher for the Comets.

For a wage-earner like Kay Heim, the promise of good money was as much a lure to the league as the chance to play professional, new-style ball. Wrigley offered players from $50 to $100 a week, depending on their age and experience. With the national wage average at $40 a week, some league players made more money than their fathers.

Charm School Girls

The excellent pay meant hard work in return. Wrigley also paid extraordinary care to the appearance and manners of the players. If he was going to put up half the cash for the new league (with the other half coming from businesses and civic groups in the four host towns), he wanted to make sure that the public got a quality product.

Though ball-playing was what the women were hired to do, Wrigley had no idea how well or consistently the All American Girls would play. Even if they showed spunk and muscle, speed and finesse, Wrigley expected that fans would be drawn to ballparks primarily by the novelty of women playing what was considered a man's sport. So he wanted to make sure that his players looked feminine and attractive.

Feminine looks and behavior wouldn't easily translate to the hot, summertime ball field. In the 1940s, women—and men too—were more formal than they are today, no matter where they were. Men usually tipped their gangster-style fedoras to women on the streets of small towns. Women wore gloves downtown to shop in department stores, and certainly, no well-brought-up young lady was seen smoking or wearing shorts or pants in public. Wrigley's scouts turned down several outstanding ballplayers because, according to *Time* magazine,

"ALWAYS appear in feminine attire when not actively engaged in practice or playing ball."

Rosie the Riveter on a Pitcher's Mound

League uniforms looked sporty, but they weren't very practical for playing baseball.

"they were either too uncouth, too hard-boiled, or too masculine."

To put forth the proper image, Wrigley put poster artist Otis Shepherd—famous for creating the Wrigley Spearmint Pixie—to work designing a uniform. League players would wear short-skirted wool dresses—in pastel colors—over heavy, cotton boxer shorts. The shorts, knee-high socks, and a hat would complement the dresses. Ann Harnett, an early recruit, modeled the first uniform for prospective players.

Wrigley also arranged for players to receive some charm school training in manners and grooming. During spring training, when they weren't sliding, batting, and sweating on Wrigley Field, the women went to the beauty salon of makeup manufacturer

Up to the Plate

Charm school graduates

Helena Rubenstein. There they learned correct posture, how to speak politely to gentlemen callers, how to cross a room in high heels, and, when sitting, to cross their feet at the ankles. Lipstick and hairdos gussied up some farm girls who had never before had a beauty-salon haircut.

Did the players like it? Some believed the makeover was necessary. "Most of us were farm girls," said pitcher Annabelle Lee, "and walked like clodhoppers." Others, like Faye Dancer, chafed at the fussy makeover: "They turned me into Buster Brown with bangs and lipstick all over me," she fumed.

That wasn't all in the feminine charm and manners department. Wrigley and his advisers hired chaperones, older women to help the players toe the line and to comfort them in times of trouble. The organizers also came up with a list of rules for ladylike conduct on and off the diamond. The rules began by distinguishing the All American Girls from their male counterparts:

WE HAVE A SPORT THAT HAS A GREAT FUTURE. GIRLS PLAYING AS MEN WOULD BE DEFINITELY IN COMPETITION WITH MEN. GIRLS PLAYING AS GIRLS OFFER A SPORT THAT HAS NO COMPETITION AND IS DESTINED TO HAVE A VERY GREAT FUTURE.

THESE GENERAL RULES ARE NECESSARY TO BUILD THE ORGANIZATION AND TO MAINTAIN ORDER IN THE CLUBS.

1. ALWAYS appear in feminine attire when not actively engaged in practice or playing ball. This regulation continues through the Shaughnessy Playoffs. At no time may a player appear in the stands in her uniform.

2. Smoking or drinking are not permitted in public places.

3. All social engagements must be approved by the chaperones.

4. All living quarters and eating places must be approved by the chaperones.

5. For emergency purposes it is necessary that you leave notice of your whereabouts at your home phone.

6. Each club will establish a satisfactory place to eat and a time when all members must be in their individual rooms. In general the lapse of time will be two hours after the finish of the last game.

7. Always carry your employee's pass as a means of identification for entering the various parks. This pass is NOT transferable.

8. Relatives, friends, and visitors are not allowed on the bench at any time.

9. Due to shortage of equipment, baseballs must not be given as souvenirs without permission of management.

10. Baseball uniform skirts shall not be shorter than six inches above the knee cap.

11. In order to sustain the complete spirit of rivalry between clubs the members of the different clubs must not fraternize at any time during the season.

12. When traveling, the members of the clubs must be at the station thirty minutes before departure time. Anyone missing her arranged transportation will have to pay her own fare.

AN AUTOMATIC FINE WILL BE IMPOSED FOR BREAKING ANY OF THE ABOVE RULES.

2

Boy! Those Girls Sure Can Play Ball

When the first teams took to South Bend's Bendix Field for the season's opening doubleheader, in late May 1943, spectators crowded the stands. Admission cost 25 cents. Philip Wrigley had been right: curiosity and hunger for cheap entertainment close to home made the teams almost instant successes in their four hometowns.

Though major-league baseball hadn't come to a halt as feared, the All American Girls had a distinctive appeal all their own. Emphasizing their patriotic calling, the players arranged themselves on the ball field in the shape of a V for "Victory," as fans sang the national anthem to start every game.

"Most of us never played in front of such big audiences before," marveled Kay Heim, as two, three, or four thousand fans showed up on occasion. In the first year of play, around 200,000 fans attended games in four cities. In the second year, nearly half a million fans attended games in six midwestern parks. These figures heartened not only Philip

Opposite page: The first four players signed to the league. Standing, from left: Clara Schillace, Ann Harnett, Edie Perlick. Seated: Shirley Jamison

Wrigley, but the businesses that sponsored the teams.

Each team was guided by a board of directors, made up of representatives from its hometown. Wrigley had also hired fatherly-type men to manage the teams, all with backgrounds in baseball or other competitive sports. Managers were supposed to work with the chaperones to give a dignified, serious atmosphere to the games. But despite the chaperones and fatherly managers, the uniform skirts and the out-of-uniform dress code, and despite expectations for fluffy, powder-puff ball, the women played from the beginning with muscle, competitive spirit, blood, and determination.

They had a hectic, nonstop schedule of ball-playing and travel. From June through August, they played seven days a week, with doubleheaders on Sundays. The first season, with a somewhat late start, lasted 108 games. It was split into two halves, with the winners of each half playing one another for the championship. As the league continued, seasons (no longer split) expanded slightly to around 112 games. A series called the Shaughnessy Playoffs—named after Francis J. Shaughnessy, an American baseball official of the early 1900s—determined the championship team.

To attract workers from defense plants, most games were played at night. In fact, on July 1, 1943, the All American Girls played the first night game ever held at Wrigley Field, under temporary lights. Film star Victor Mature threw out the first ball and helped draw some 7,000 fans. But though the players were thrilled, the audience did not impress Wrigley and his advisers, who decided Chicagoans were not ready for a league team of their own.

A few teams played on converted football fields. Otherwise, softball fields were used, with the distances between bases and the pitcher's mound altered. Like Wrigley Field, a couple of hometown parks didn't have lights. But as the league began to prosper, city business leaders installed them. During the day, the teams either practiced long

To prove that players were "ladylike," publicity photos showed the All American Girls doing laundry and applying makeup.

hours on the field or traveled. When the women did manage an excursion downtown, fans stopped them in the streets, and if the players didn't respond with friendly banter, the fans would give them a ribbing from the stands that evening.

In more ways than one, the players belonged to the towns that supported their teams with enthusiasm and dollars. With the approval of the chaperone, the women roomed in the homes of local residents. Some kindly but uninterested landladies offered the players midnight snacks of milk and cookies but never saw them play. Other hometown supporters became ardent fans and lifelong friends. During the war years, fans gave players rationing coupons, which enabled them to buy extra limited items like butter and meat. Fans entertained the players' fiancés or invited the whole team to lake cabins or farms for wiener roasts, boating, or horseback riding. Though romance was certainly a topic of interest—the league players were, after all, mainly in their teens and twenties—the schedule of travel and games, and the strict rules of conduct, left little time for dating.

Manager Marty McManus gives some big-league advice to Kenosha pitchers Mary Pratt, Helen Nicol Fox, and Lee Harvey.

Up to the Plate

Writers and photographers followed the All American Girls to spring training.

Publicity photos, which did not reflect reality, showed players applying lipstick on the field or giving each other fancy hairdos after hours. But rare was the player who actually whipped out a compact on second base and freshened up her makeup. In fact, by the second night of play, *Time* magazine reported, "some of the polish [had worn] thin. Despite Helena Rubenstein and Mr. Wrigley, two of the ladies got into a fish-wife argument that nearly ended in a fist fight."

Still, looking feminine and attractive was part of the contract. With the hard physical work of ballplaying, and sometimes living out of suitcases, the players found it difficult to maintain a glamorous image. "I was always putting my hair up in curlers," complained Joyce Hill, a rookie catcher in 1945. "We'd sweat out on the field all morning, then come home to shower and change for the night games. My hair never had enough curl."

Keeping a wardrobe looking decent was also not as high a priority for the players as it was for the league's organizers. When the schedule was tight, the teams traveled all night, leaving the ballparks with suitcases already packed. They took "night

Batters didn't always agree with the umpire's call.

flyers" into Chicago, where they'd change trains, sometimes kicking suitcases down the sidewalk at three in the morning. The trains were sooty and crowded. Servicemen got priority seating.

The minute they got into their hotel rooms, the women turned on hot showers full blast to let the steam take the wrinkles out of skirts and dresses. "This was in the era before permanent press," recalled pitcher Dottie Wiltse.

Dressing for the games was also problematic. The league uniforms, with their short skirts, boxer shorts, and kneesocks, drew attention on streets and city buses. On the field, players sometimes found themselves trapped or limited by the uniforms. So they improvised. In the early years of the league, when pitchers used the underhand, windmill style from fast-pitch softball, many quickly discovered that their flared skirts interfered with their delivery. Annabelle Lee, a southpaw, took a tuck in her skirt to remove some of the bulky fabric. She went on to pitch a perfect game (no opponent reached first base) for her first-year team.

Sliding into base, always exciting, posed an extra danger of bruised flesh and bloody skin. Short skirts left large areas of thigh exposed to hard ground, cleats, and rough play. Surveying Horlick Field in Racine, Kurys said, "That's where I shed a lot of blood." Few were the players who didn't sport a "strawberry" or two. Thigh scrapes and bruises, patched up with antiseptic, gauze, and white tape by concerned teammates or chaperones, became a badge of courage. Some players made sliding pads out of pieces of mattress pad and pinned them inside their shorts. Philip Wrigley certainly didn't intend for the young women to play injured, but he

Lefty Annabelle Lee (above). Short skirts made sliding home (right) treacherous.

Boy! Those Girls Sure Can Play Ball

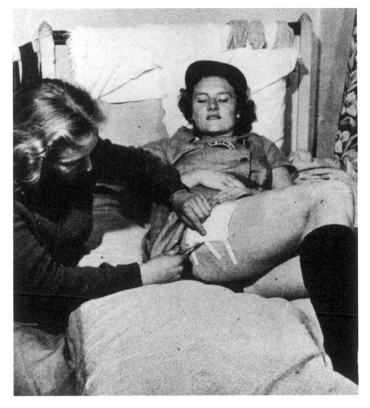

Thelma Eisen patches up teammate Faye Dancer.

hadn't foreseen their determination, stamina, competitiveness, and verve when he had chosen the uniform.

A number of first-year players carried their early skill and enthusiasm into many years of play. Dorothy Kamenshek of the Rockford Peaches was headed for a career as an outstanding first sacker and would lead the league on and off for years in hits, runs scored, batting percentage, and times at bat. Ex-Yankee first baseman Wally Pipp called her the best fielder he'd ever seen. In 1950 she was offered, but declined, a minor-league tryout.

Sophie Kurys would amass 1,114 stolen bases in her nine years of play. Had she been a man, that number would no doubt have earned her a spot in the Baseball Hall of Fame. Betsy Jochum, a South Bend Blue Sox, led the league in hits for 1943 (120) and 1944 (128) and led the league in singles during the same years with 100 and 120. Shortstop Dottie

Schroeder, also a Blue Sox, stayed with the league through its entire history. She impressed Chicago Cubs manager Charlie Grimm so much that he said he'd pay $50,000 for her, "if only she were a man."

—— *Managers and Players* —— *Tune Up the Game*

Hired to help the teams achieve professional skill on the field, managers selected by Philip Wrigley and his staff sometimes did and sometimes did not advance the women's games. Initially, Wrigley hired managers with famous names. Belles' manager Johnny Gottselig was a hockey star and an off-season softball manager in Canada. The other three first-year managers were Bert Niehoff for the South Bend Blue Sox, a six-year major league infielder; Josh Billings for the Kenosha Comets, an outfielder with 11 years in the majors; and Eddie Stumpf for the Rockford Peaches, a former minor-league catcher.

Since neither Wrigley, his advisers, nor the boards of directors of the four teams realized how fierce the play would be, the managers saw their role—at the beginning at least—more as kindly father figures than as hardworking, competitive leaders.

Without strong management in the first year, how did the players perform? Though reluctant to attach blame to any particular manager, some players hint that they were the ones who initially showed managers, fans, boosters, and backers how well they could play the game. With base paths at 60 feet—5 feet longer than in softball—and the distance from home plate to the pitching mound lengthened from 35 to 40 feet, the women developed a unique game.

It was still, like fast-pitch softball, very much a pitcher's game. The number of hits was low, averaging around 12.5 per game, compared to 18 for major-league baseball. League pitchers usually

Joanne Winter winds up.

*Annabelle Lee pitches
her way into the record
books.*

"went the distance," pitching all nine innings. During the 1944 season, three Racine Belle pitchers—Mary Crews, Jane Jacobs, and Joanne Winter—together went 39 consecutive games without relief.

Games often stretched into extra innings, as pitchers dueled it out with low-scoring ties. One game Kay Heim caught for Kenosha lasted 18 innings. Her knees didn't bother her as much as her arm: "I thought I'd never throw again," she said, the catcher being the player who receives and returns the ball the most.

With the softball's sluggish performance in the air, the women discovered that stealing bases was a glorious opportunity. In other words, they could outrun the ball. Sophie Kurys stole 44 bases the first year, and her total ballooned to 166 the second. Though her performance was outstanding, she was not alone. Teammates and competitors alike stole bases like deer outrunning hunters. Catchers and fielders simply couldn't push the heavy, fat softball through the air fast enough to bring the runners down.

The first year, the Racine Belles won the first half of the season, Kenosha the second. After some excessive celebrating, a group of Comets almost landed in Lake Michigan, driving their Model-T Ford off the road in a fog. They escaped unharmed, though, and then played the Belles for the championship. Five games were scheduled, but only three were necessary for Racine to whomp the Comets. The Belles brought home 60 percent of the gate receipts, a flag, a plaque for city hall, and a $1,000 scholarship to the University of Wisconsin for a high school girl, according to league president Ken Sells, "to encourage athletics among women for health and recreation."

— Expansion Teams: Boom or Bust —

Fans cheered and hooted, and players yelled back at them.

Enthusiastic about the first year's performance of his brainchild, Philip Wrigley brought 250 feet of film from a Racine game to the winter meetings of major- and minor-league baseball in New York. Major-league baseball didn't seem to need a patriotic substitute after all, but Wrigley hoped the film of the All American Girls would impress officials, club owners, umpires, sportswriters, and baseball players.

Though the boast that the All American Girls were on their way to being a "third major league" was mostly a proud father's pipe dream, Wrigley was able to persuade two cities that new women's teams would help fill their minor-league parks with fans. Minneapolis, Minnesota, and Milwaukee, Wisconsin, invited Wrigley to organize teams, the Minneapolis Millerettes (named after a men's team called the Millers) and the Milwaukee Chicks. Wrigley was so sure that the league would prosper that he agreed to support the two new teams completely, without financial backing from local businesses.

California Hopefuls

During the league's second season, scouts turned up a passel of California players, reared in the Los Angeles fast-pitch softball leagues. The California players were used to attention. They wore skintight satin shorts and played before movie stars and directors. Dottie Wiltse once shot a publicity photo (left) with film star Jeffrey Lynn (of *Million Dollar Baby*), and her teammate Kay Rohrer had been given a screen test. "The movie people thought if you could perform on a ball diamond, you might have star quality," remembered Wiltse. She never made it to a screen test; her teeth weren't quite straight enough for the movies.

The Milwaukee Chicks started out with manager Max Carey, a hall-of-famer noted for stealing bases. He had managed the Brooklyn Dodgers before he agreed to lead the new All American Girls team. At one point, a Milwaukee newspaper dubbed the team the "Schnitts" or "Little Brews," references to the city's German sausage and beer tradition. But with Carey as manager, another name, based on a book titled *Mother Carey's Chickens,* suggested itself.

Under Carey's leadership, the Chicks played the 1944 season to an outstanding finale. The Kenosha Comets won the first half of the season, but the Milwaukee team staged an 11-game winning streak in August to take the second half. The playoffs required a full seven-game series to complete.

The second new team, the Minneapolis Millerettes, fared much worse than its other big-city

*Manager Claude
Jonnard and chaperone
Ada Ryan (far left and far
right) guided the
Millerettes through a
rocky season.*

cousin. Minneapolis's minor-league men's team
had recently been staffed with a new manager and
players. And the city's business leaders and sportswriters gave only halfhearted attention to the new
female players at Nicollet Park. The Minneapolis
Tribune ran a photo of a local player, but no story.
Then, popular sportscaster and columnist Halsey Hall delivered a condescending introduction a
week before the Millerettes opened: "Common cour-
tesy and the sweet little niceties accorded ladies
generally go by the boards at Nicollet Park next
weekend."

On opening day, May 27, a writer from United
Press let loose a flurry of humor and fake horror:
"Quick, Millie, my mask and mascara, for there's a
powder-puff plot under way...aimed at virtual ex-
tinction of the perspiring, swearing, tobacco-chew-
ing baseball player." In the accompanying photo,
Dottie Wiltse leaned into a vigorous toss, but the
sportswriter chose to see the players as charm
school graduates rather than good athletes.

The manager chosen for the Millerettes was
Claude Jonnard, who had pitched six years for the

Giants, the Cardinals, and the White Sox and had led the National League in games pitched in 1923. Jonnard didn't take the women's game very seriously and, as Dottie Wiltse said, didn't push the team very much. California native Faye Dancer criticized the manager more strongly: "I loved the sport," she said. "I wanted to play to win. Jonnard was always negative. We California girls made up our own signals and played our own game."

The Millerettes' opening game was a minor disappointment, with the California-bred trio of Wiltse, Faye Dancer, and Pepper Paire limiting the Rockford Peaches to a one-run win at 5-4. Halsey Hall was impressed. "Chatter was the only feminine touch to the proceedings," he wrote. "In a welter of flaring skirts, headlong and feet-first slides...bodily contact, good pitching, and really brilliant outfielding," the Millerettes performed like genuine ballplayers, with Dancer a "fly-catching genius." The team seemed ready to go the full season.

Visiting teams from smaller towns enjoyed the big city excitement. They hung their laundered underwear in the windows of the Sheraton Hotel and received a huffy reprimand from the front desk. They paid a quarter to sit in a velvet pew at St. Olaf's church for Sunday services, and, ignoring the rule against socializing with the opposition, ate frog legs with women from rival clubs at Charlie's Cafe Exceptionale.

Not everything was so much fun. "We'd put on our uniforms and ride to Nicollet Field on the streetcar, a bit embarrassing in short skirts," remembered Kay Heim. But that was a minor inconvenience compared to the size of the field. When the scaled-down women's game was played in the big minor-league park, hitting a home run was nearly impossible, fielding a long fly could take precious extra seconds, and, perhaps most frustrating of all, fans couldn't enjoy the kind of intimacy available at smaller fields.

Despite Faye Dancer's antics on the field—cartwheels on her way out to play, handstands while waiting for a hit—fans weren't as closely involved

*Lavonne "Pepper" Paire
gets set to catch.*

in the game as the women would have liked. "At Racine, Kenosha, South Bend, or Rockford, the fans could almost reach out and touch us," explained Dottie Wiltse. They could easily talk to the players and watch the blood fly when Dancer slid into base with her famous hook slide that put bare skin to the dirt.

The cost of transporting teams all the way across Wisconsin to Minneapolis also mounted up, and directors from the smaller towns began to complain to Philip Wrigley. The Millerettes, who led the league for a while, soon began to lose. Annabelle Lee's exciting perfect game was not played at home, and by the end of July, with local news coverage shrunk to the bottom corners of back pages, the Millerettes had fallen to last place.

In Racine and Kenosha, South Bend and Rockford, big crowds had become commonplace, and local papers touted the players' efforts with tall headlines. The businesses that supported the teams prospered. But in Minneapolis, games were poorly attended. Wrigley financed the women's team himself, while local businesses put their money into two minor-league men's teams instead.

Near the end of the 1944 season, the Millerettes were told that they were traveling to Milwaukee for two days. But in fact, the league pulled up stakes from Minneapolis and turned the Millerettes into a touring team called the Orphans. "All our clothes were left behind," complained Annabelle Lee. "We had to buy boys' T-shirts, anything that didn't have to be ironed." The players were young and resilient, and they'd do almost anything to keep playing. But the departure from Minneapolis left them disappointed.

Even for the Milwaukee Chicks in their winning season, the big minor-league park was not as well suited to the women's game as were the smaller softball fields. In addition, teams in small towns had less entertainment competition than did those in big cities, and business leaders were willing to stake local funds and encourage fans to come to the games.

By far the most rebellious of the All American Girls, Faye Dancer was almost as famous for breaking the rules as she was for her ball-playing skills.

The 1944 season saw a turning point in World War II. On D day, June 6, thousands of troops from the United States and its allies stormed beaches in Normandy, France. The Allies were close to victory, and fewer American men were being drafted into the military. Major-league baseball clearly was not going to shut down. Some professional players had been discharged from the service and were returning to their teams. After the 1944 season, Philip Wrigley decided to withdraw from the All American Girls League and devote all of his energy and funds to the Chicago Cubs.

During the winter, representatives of the four original women's teams met in Chicago. Arthur Meyerhoff, a lawyer and friend of Wrigley's, proposed a new plan for operating the league. He suggested that the local boards of directors take over supervision of the teams and that representatives from each club form a governing body to guide the organization. Wrigley turned over all the league's assets to the boards of directors, Meyerhoff took charge of the reorganization, and Max Carey was named the league's new president.

Two new cities expressed interest in hosting a team. Thus, the Orphans were adopted by Fort Wayne, Indiana, and became the Fort Wayne Daisies. The Milwaukee Chicks crossed Lake Michigan and moved to Grand Rapids, Michigan, retaining their name as the Grand Rapids Chicks. Now the league looked forward to its third season, ready to show doubters that women's professional ball could succeed without Wrigley's promotional backing and partial subsidy.

3

On the Way to the Top

By 1945, when the All American Girls League was clearly going strong, the job of training, planning lineups, keeping up morale, going nose to nose with the umpires, and generally making the teams competitive no longer fell to the players themselves. Managers took a more active role in coaching.

"Come on, Dottie, get a hit or get hit," Rockford manager Bill Allington would yell at Dottie Ferguson, his leadoff hitter. "He used to call me Slugger," Ferguson recalls, "because he could count on me to get on base." Like Allington, many managers stayed around for years, switching from team to team as they were needed.

Still very much a pitcher's league in 1945, the All American Girls pushed back the base paths from 60 to 68 feet and the mound-to-home plate distance from 40 to 42 feet. The league also dropped the size of the ball from 12 to 11½ inches in circumference. Intended to increase the liveliness of the ball and give the hitters an advantage, these changes, in fact, did not affect the game very much.

Opposite page: A disagreement at home plate

Home runs actually dropped. In 1943 Ellie Dapkus of the Racine Belles had led the league with 10; in 1945 leaders Helen Callaghan and Faye Dancer of the Fort Wayne Daisies had 3 each. The best league batting average also fell each year: from .332, posted by Rockford Peach Gladys Davis in 1943, to .299, earned by Helen Callaghan in 1945. A new statistic, total advanced bases, was introduced in 1945 to record the number of bases that batters advanced other runners. With a tremendous margin over other players, Helen Callaghan also led in this department, with 336 TABs that year.

By 1945 the league teams began to put out yearbooks, published jointly by town businesses and local booster groups. Not surprisingly, the 1945 Player of the Year, Grand Rapids Chicks ace pitcher Connie Wisniewski, was honored with a large spread in her team's yearbook. She was so formidable, in fact, that one sportswriter declared that she was really two pitchers, one named "Weis" and the other named "Newski." In 1945 Wisniewski shared with Joanne Winter of the Racine Belles the distinction of winning 33 games in a season. Wisniewski also led the league that year in won-lost percentage

The 1945 South Bend Blue Sox

Tommy Thompson (foreground) jokes with teammates in the Grand Rapids dressing room.

at .786 and kept batters to an amazingly low earned run average of 0.81 runs per game. With Dottie Wiltse of Fort Wayne, Helen Nicol Fox of Kenosha, and Charlotte Armstrong of South Bend, she shared the most games pitched, at 46. Alone, Wisniewski pitched the most innings, 391. (No one pitched more than 313 innings in the major leagues that year, despite the majors' season going 44 games longer.)

The downside to such big numbers was the exhaustion and injury suffered by many pitching staffs. Reviewing the 1945 season, the Racine Belles' yearbook described a desperation move of pitcher Mary Crews to the outfield, where she tore a shoulder ligament diving for a smash hit. With Crews injured, the Belles pitching staff was reduced to Winter and Jane Jacobs. These two had to work alternate games, and sometimes pitched six to eight games in a stretch.

Finally, in June, Racine obtained pitcher Doris Barr from South Bend, but three other Racine players then proceeded to injure thighs, knees, or ankles. Sophie Kurys's base-stealing total was kept

Mickey Maguire bats for the Chicks.

to 115 that year because of an injury. No wonder the Belles found themselves in the cellar at mid-season.

A Legendary Series

Incessant rain around Lake Michigan added gloom to Racine's burden. The Belles were scheduled for a series of games against the Grand Rapids Chicks. But in a downpour of legendary proportions, they were stuck in hotel rooms in Grand Rapids for three days, as the ballpark filled with water.

Racine sports announcer and humorist Don Black wrote in the yearbook that Grand Rapids manager Benny "Sea Horse" Meyer was eager to start the series because he saw so many Belles on crutches. But every time he visited the ballpark, to paraphrase Black, he returned with his voice waterlogged and a pond of water in his ears. (No one thought to dry out the bases and pitcher's mound with a blow torch, as a Kenosha Comets ground crew had done one evening on the other side of Lake Michigan.)

Finally the soggy series started. Manager Meyer boasted, "We will swamp them Belles." The Chicks proceeded to do just that, 2-0 in the first game. A well-padded umpire named Rimes clogged the route to second base, and in the second game, when he moved to the plate, he soon displayed "a strange habit of calling balls strikes and the strikes vice-versa." The managers converged to chew him out, and in the commotion, the batting order got mixed up three times.

Eventually the Belles broke through the great Wisniewski's pitching for a couple of hits, putting Irene Hickson on third and Edie Perlick on second. With Clara "Twinkletoes" Schillace at bat, Meyer signaled Wisniewski to walk her. Unfortunately, Chicks catcher Mickey Maguire missed one of the pitches, and while she chased down the ball, Irene Hickson ran in from third to the plate. Maguire got the ball and let it fly, but the ball conked Hickson on the head as she slid toward the plate, which she tagged, according to Don Black, "with the end of her nose." Meanwhile, Edie Perlick kept coming from second, scored a run, and joined the group escorting Hickson to the bench. When the mud was cleared off the plate, the umpire decided that the count on Schillace was four balls and three strikes. Since that was impossible, Schillace got a free walk to first base, and the Belles drove her home for the third run of the game.

Yet, when the inning was over, the scoreboard displayed only two runs for the Belles instead of three. Apparently the umpire, official scorer, and announcer were all too busy eyeing "Tuffy Hickson lying prone in the dust" to notice that Edie Perlick had crossed the plate. Fans and Belles certified that she had, and the run was credited to Racine. Then, in the bottom of the ninth, with the score tied at 4-4, one out, and the bases loaded with Chicks, the next batter hit the ball to Racine

"Believe me, it's something. Those girls play real ball."

infielder Joanne Winter. Winter threw to the catcher, Hickson, which forced the runner from third out at the plate. Hickson then rifled the ball to first base to complete a snappy double play and retire the side. Grand Rapids Chicks were already charging the field for the first extra inning when the umpire ruled that Hickson had not had her foot on the plate when she caught the throw, thus the runner had scored and the game was over.

This started a free-for-all that made the three days of thunder and lightning sound like a mere pitter-pat. The Belles stormed the umpire, and fans seconded. A few Grand Rapids fans heckled Belle Ellie Dapkus to be a good sport, and she offered to bash in their heads. "When we left the park," mused Don Black, "several of the Belles were missing, having hitch-hiked to town on the umpire's neck."

All in all, it was one of the liveliest tall-tale losses in ball-playing history. As the yearbook said, "the Belles pulled a fast double play to apparently retire the side, only to have the umpire reverse the decision to cost them the game."

South Bend Blue Sox

1945 YEAR BOOK

25¢

—— *Rivalries and Romance* ——

Since things could not get much worse for the Belles, they got better. Halfway through the 1945 season, new manager Leo Murphy and new chaperone Mildred "Willie" Wilson came on board. Wilson brought a charming personality and a firm hand to her job. A softball catcher and manager, and also a basketball star, she knew how to have fun. When the players were asked to do a radio talk show, she added her voice to theirs. She took their pictures at swimming parties and joined them to visit a hospitalized bat boy. She could also be very businesslike. She helped players escape from "locker-room Lotharios" (amorous male fans) and politely decline dinner invitations. The league code of behavior was strict, but Wilson understood that being friendly and helpful to the team was more important than riding the rules.

Leo Murphy had been a Racine fan from the beginning and had served on the team's board of strategy, a companion board to the directors. With 25 years of ball-playing experience, mostly in midwestern minor leagues, he coached the Belles out of the cellar to fourth place at the end of the season. Though the Belles lost in the first round of the Shaughnessy Playoffs against Fort Wayne, the switch in manager and chaperone got them on solid footing for the following year. They would go on to have the best record in the league and then win the playoff crown.

Before that could happen, however, the 1945 championship was played between Rockford and Fort Wayne. By this time, the top four teams in the league paired off and played against each other in a best-of-five series. The winners played another best-of-five series for the top prize. The Rockford Peaches were pitched to the championship largely by Carolyn Morris. In four of her six wins, Morris won by a margin of only one run. Though Kay Rohrer hit two triples for the Peaches in the final series, the playoffs were won by pitching and fielding. Rockford committed only 8 errors in the nine playoff games, compared to 23 for Fort Wayne. And rookie Dottie Ferguson tallied up an impressive fielding average of .961 at second base, third in the league.

While the teams hustled on the field, some players found that private life simply wouldn't wait till the off-season. By August 1945, the Fort Wayne Daisies had caught on big in their new hometown. One of the star attractions was pitcher Dottie Wiltse.

During one Sunday doubleheader, serviceman Harvey Collins sat in the stands while Wiltse pitched. His friend, an avid Daisies fan, regularly bought each winning pitcher a case of beer. As Dottie polished off one game and went on to win the next, Harvey and his friend cooked up a scheme to visit Dottie and her roommates, all Daisies, after the game.

Harvey was intrigued by Dottie. She resembled a

Some fans sat in the same spot every night, heckling players who were lagging, cheering those having a good game.

female pitcher he'd seen on the other side of the world—in a newspaper photo pasted on the inside of a serviceman's locker on Johnston Island, in the middle of the Pacific Ocean. Now in Fort Wayne, as he sat in an upstairs apartment surrounded by Faye Dancer, Tex Lessing, Vivian Kellogg, Pepper Paire, and of course Dottie, Harvey tried to figure out how his buddy in the Pacific had acquired a photo of one ball-playing California girl, while here he was, meeting another.

With that question on his mind, Harvey asked Dottie on a golfing date. One thing led to another, and soon they were sneaking around together, trying to outsmart the chaperone and manager Bill Wambsganss. Harvey eventually flipped through Dottie's scrapbook and identified the same newspaper photo that he'd seen in his buddy's locker. It showed Dottie's California friend Barbara White, wearing the satin softball uniform of the Payne Furnace Company team, which she and Dottie had played for in 1940.

At the end of the season, Dottie Wiltse pitched the Daisies into the final series, but she could not stop the Peaches from winning the championship. The loss was a disappointment, but it didn't keep Harvey and Dottie, along with teammate Helen Callaghan, from whooping it up on a long drive across the country to California. Harvey had three days to report back to Camp Shoemaker.

In South Dakota, they stopped to attend a dance with some of Dottie's friends. With a deadline of midnight for his arrival in California, Harvey telegraphed his base that his car had broken down. Expecting the worst, he reported three days late. But instead of being court-martialed, he was given a 30-day leave in California. World War II was over. An armistice had been signed in both Europe and the Pacific, and military personnel were slowly returning to civilian life.

In March 1946, Dottie married Harvey Collins in California, with her friend Barbara White as matron of honor. Dottie returned to the Daisies in 1946 and pitched 16 strikeouts in one game. But

Dottie Wiltse was a hit in Fort Wayne.

*War's end would bring
changes to American
society and to female
ballplayers.*

her living arrangements changed. She moved out of the apartment she had shared with Faye Dancer and four other players and left them to handle the sink heaped with dishes, the unmade beds, and piles of dirty clothes. By this time, a number of women in the league had also married and continued to play.

— Hitting the Road after the War —

With the war over and gas rationing lifted, the teams began to travel on private buses rather than trains. This meant players could have more privacy after a night under the lights, seats to themselves, and a chance to sing favorite old songs and Pepper

Paire's new league anthem. Some women played cards or read, some slept, and some sat up front to guide the driver into rival towns in the dark.

The women could ride the bus in slacks. But if they wanted to get off, even to use the restroom, they had to change into skirts, comb their hair, and touch up their lipstick. Some fussy chaperones even insisted that they remain on the bus until their hotel rooms had been searched for enthusiastic fans who might have followed them on the road.

Mishaps sometimes occurred on the highways. Players were late packing their luggage and ran frantically after the departing bus. If they were left behind, they had to find their own transportation to the rival town for the next game, and they might be fined by the league. In the days before superhighways and high-speed vehicles, players spent a lot of time on the bus.

In 1946 two new teams joined the league, the Muskegon (Michigan) Lassies and the Peoria (Illinois) Red Wings. Peoria officials first heard about the league from general manager Fred Avery, who arranged for businesspeople, civic leaders, and sportswriters to travel to Rockford for a game.

The Blue Sox enjoy an outing at Joyce Hill's family farm.

Rockford manager Bill Allington joined the Peoria visitors in the stands. The doubleheader played to a sellout crowd.

The mixture of fast-paced ball and the big crowd appealed to the Peoria sponsors, and soon they were convinced, said the team's yearbook, that "the game of Girls Baseball, as played in the All-American League, was strictly as represented—thrilling, of major league calibre, and the type of high-class summer time entertainment that Peoria so badly needed."

With a start-up fund of $21,000 raised from city merchants, and with a manager—local favorite Wild Bill Rodgers from the old-time Three-I (Illinois, Iowa, Indiana) League—the sponsors only needed a name for the team. So they held a contest. Red Wings won, Arrows came in second, and Indianas was third. The Peoria Stadium, home of high school football, was altered for women's baseball by placing home plate in front of the right end of the grandstand and adding bleachers down the first-base line to the right-field wire fence. The dimensions of the field were irregular, with a short hop to the right-field fence, but a vast distance in left field. To add light for night games, two power poles were placed behind home plate. A handful of veterans, including Annabelle Lee, Kay Blumetta, Ann Harnett, and Thelma Eisen, joined a host of newcomers chosen at the 1946 spring training in Pascagoula, Mississippi.

By leaving the Chicago area for spring training, the league hoped to gather fans from other parts of the country. Few people outside the Midwest had seen the All American Girls play. In Mississippi, organizers thought, the league might also attract local players to try out. The war had disrupted the widespread network of softball teams that had initially trained many league players. Wartime blackouts on both coasts made night softball games difficult. Now that the league was growing, finding full-fledged recruits was becoming harder. The league planned to send pairs of teams to barnstorm, or play exhibition games, throughout the

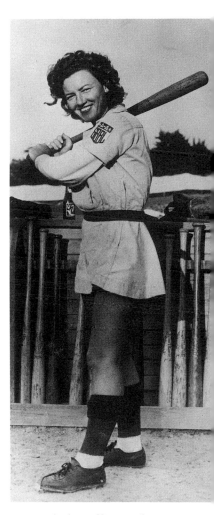

Despite the efforts of seasoned players like Annabelle Lee, Peoria struggled in its first year.

South. This would encourage interest in the sport and plant the idea of playing in the minds of more young women.

Spring training in Pascagoula had a few surprises for northern women. "Roach heaven," many called it. The few Southerners already in the league laughed at their teammates' squeamishness. "It's just a l'il ole roach," they teased. But to the Northerners, the sight of a roach an inch long was a signal to grab a shoe for the kill.

Once the Red Wings were settled in Peoria, fans were slow in coming—typical of other new teams' first few weeks. The first game, played on May 26 in chilly weather, produced a good showing, with Annabelle Lee pitching the Red Wings to a 7-0, six-hit win over the Kenosha Comets. But after that, the Red Wings played in last place (33 wins, 79 losses) the whole season, despite a change in manager to Johnny Gottselig halfway through.

Marnie Danhauser patrolled first base for the Racine Belles.

The most exciting ball was probably played by Thelma Eisen, called "the Ty Cobb of women's baseball." Rivaling Sophie Kurys, she stole 128 bases, hit .256, and hit the only two home runs managed that year by the Red Wings.

Fans finally arrived in encouraging numbers, with total attendance reaching 68,000 for the season, a figure, crowed the yearbook, that "even the most optimistic were forced to marvel at. Here was a novel venture in the field of sports, introduced into an admittedly indifferent city, mired in last place in the League and eyed with skepticism from its inception, drawing more than 68,000 fans in one season!"

Total attendance at league games in 1946 reached 754,000 in the eight cities, triple the number of three years before. Racine set an all-time record for its four years—probably not a surprise, as the Racine Belles held the season lead early and landed the championship at the end.

The South Bend Blue Sox had moved from Bendix Field, where the commercial men's softball team played, to an amusement park named Playland. A roller skating rink, swimming pool, fairgrounds, and auto racetrack vied with the women's games for audience attention. Fans from South Bend were noted for their enthusiasm, however. One Blue Sox fan gave prizes of silver dollars, war bonds, radios, and record players to batters who hit doubles or triples. Even at Playland, the All American Girls beat out the other competition for audiences and chalked up a single-game record of more than 7,800 fans.

Blue Sox Mona Denton and Joyce Hill at the entrance to Playland

The league had more than caught on. It was not just a wartime stopgap, but by 1946 was established as a spirited and popular enterprise that gave all signs of continuing. More people than ever had a chance to hear about the league when Racine radio station WRJN started play-by-play broadcasting of many home and road games. Newspaper coverage continued to be thorough in the hometowns, with writers among the more familiar spectators in the parks.

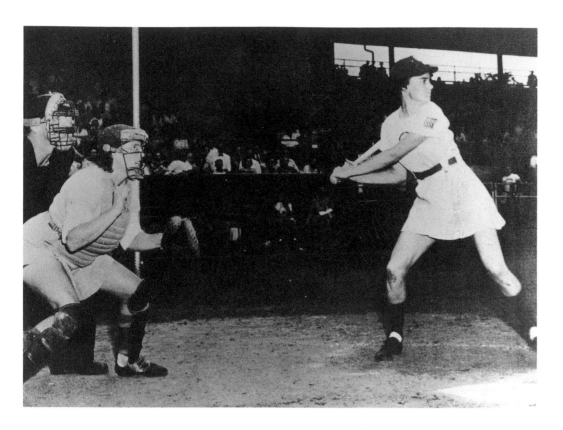

—————— A Game for Pitchers ——————
and Runners

By this time, anyone who followed the league knew the game differed from standard baseball and softball. In 1946 the baselines were again extended—from 68 to 70 feet—and the home plate to pitcher's mound length from 42 to 43 feet. The ball decreased a bit in size to 11 inches, but its weight of $5\frac{1}{8}$ ounces was only a fraction more than the men's baseball at 5 ounces. The smaller ball was intended to benefit hitters, and indeed batting averages generally edged up during the season.

Some pitchers (15 out of 40) also began to experiment with sidearm delivery, observing the rule that "the pitching hand should pass the body no higher than the belt line." Most underhand, windmill hurlers didn't alter their practice (the top four pitchers in the league still pitched windmill style). But some newcomers, and veterans with less success at pitching, were glad to try the sidearm technique.

The championship playoffs showed once again how vital the pitchers were to winning games. As the Rockford Peaches and Racine Belles battled in the last game of the five-game series, Belles pitcher Joanne Winter "was not in trouble occasionally; she was in trouble all the time," one sportswriter declared. Rockford players kept crowding the bases, but "she kept them on the bags when the chips were down." No one scored.

Rockford's Carolyn Morris pitched a no-hit game for nine innings, but finally, in the 10th, the Belles knocked two hits off of her. She was replaced in the 12th by Millie Deegan. Run-downs kept runners

A close call at home plate

from reaching home, and one player made a spectacular catch: she turned as the ball was hit, leaped in the air, and caught the ball with her back to home plate. The score held at 0-0.

In the 14th inning, Sophie Kurys, who had been on base three times previously and had stolen four bases, "singled through the left side of [the] Rockford infield." She stole second, her fifth base of the evening. Then, "with the infield drawn in for a bunt, little Betty Trezza drove a sharp grounder through the right side of the infield into right field, and Kurys rounded third, raced the throw to the plate, and won the race with a dive that carried her across with the winning run." The score was 1-0, Racine Belles win.

The All American Girls game was a running game, as league president Max Carey emphasized. In 1946 Sophie Kurys ran away with base after base, totaling 201 stolen bases that year for a league record. The 1946 Player of the Year award

Managers at spring training. Many retired major-leaguers lent their baseball experience to the All American Girls.

Connie Mack (sixth from left), called the best baseball manager of all time, visits with the Kenosha Comets.

went to Kurys, not only for her record of stolen bases, but also for a record number of runs scored, 119; 93 bases on balls; a second-place batting average of .286; 5 runs in one game; and a fielding percentage of .973 at second base. To attain her fielding record, she had 295 putouts, 239 assists, and only 15 errors.

When the league's first All-Star team was named, Sophie Kurys was on it, along with 12 other players. The idea originated with Racine's Don Black, who wrote for the nationally distributed publication *Major League Baseball Facts and Figures*. Black had league managers vote for an All-Star team, and the 1946 edition of the publication featured pictures and statistics about the All American Girls.

4

Ten Teams and a Million Fans

What did the ballplayers do in the off-season? When the war was on, many worked in defense plants, like the Nash aircraft factory in Kenosha and the Briggs airplane engine plant in Detroit. Some went home to work in card shops, service stations, or dry-cleaning establishments. Others taught school or coached local amateur teams.

Back home in California, Annabelle Lee practiced playing ball alongside major-league teams in training. Other league players stayed in the midwestern towns where their teams spent the summers. Lib Mahon was traded from the Kenosha Comets to the South Bend Blue Sox in 1945 and landed a job teaching at South Bend's Jefferson School. When the teaching and ball-playing seasons overlapped, her seventh-graders sometimes came to watch her work toward league-leading totals for 1946 with the most total advanced bases, 326, and the most runs batted in, 72.

Opposite page: On a special trip to Cuba, players and managers descend the steps of the University of Havana.

But in 1947, spring training took Mahon so far from home that many of her students hadn't even heard of the place: Havana, Cuba. Arranged in the days when the United States was friendly with the Cuban government, the Havana spring training was the idea of league president Max Carey and a Cuban friend who managed a women's ball club, las Cubanas.

The chance to travel out of the United States, especially to the warmth and hospitality of Cuba, appealed to many All American players. They took the train to Miami, where they boarded a two-propeller plane for the overseas flight. The small plane flew low and encountered a lot of turbulence. "I'd never get on a little plane like that now," one player said many years later.

Once arrived, the players stayed at the Seville Biltmore Hotel in the heart of Havana, with a view of the beautiful blue harbor. Pathe News, an American newsreel service, documented all eight teams, in uniform, running down the many-tiered steps of the ornate University of Havana. Folks back home who'd never heard of the league suddenly were introduced to them in a foreign setting.

Above: Mrs. America (Tommy Thompson's sister) accompanied the league to Cuba and attracted lots of attention. Right: tropical fruit was a special treat for the All American visitors.

Isabel Alvares had a different view of the special visitors to Cuba. She was already there, a 13-ycar-old pitcher for las Cubanas. Isabel's mother was her inspiration and main fan. A devoted follower of Cuban men's teams, Señora Alvares listened to the games on the radio and lit candles for the ballplayers. When she realized that Isabel had ball-playing talent, she asked a neighbor to train her and later took her to the home of las Cubanas' manager to try out. He gave Isabel a slot on the team.

Las Cubanas were modeled after the All American Girls. Even their uniforms had the same short skirts worn over shorts. When the Americans arrived, they played several exhibition games against las Cubanas in the Havana stadium where the Dodgers trained.

"The Cubans loved watching the girls play," remembered South Bend Blue Sox Betsy Jochum.

Las Cubanas cheer their teammates from the dugout.

Drinking was forbidden, but these Racine Belles managed to enjoy a few bottles of beer at Sloppy Joe's Bar in Havana.

The Cuban-U.S. games drew larger crowds than the Dodgers usually did in their spring training, and a year later, las Cubanas toured with the league All-Stars to South America. Isabel Alvares had to wait until 1949, when she was 15, to come to the United States and land a place in the All American League.

On the streets of Havana, the All American Girls enjoyed shopping for pineapples and mangoes and attracting small followings of shoe-shine boys. Many sunbathed on the roof of the hotel, and some got nasty burns in the hot tropical sun. Hardly any of the players liked the strong Cuban coffee. Lib Mahon was depressed by the poverty she saw: "In Cuba people were either wealthy or poor. I saw a lot of little children wearing only torn T-shirts."

When May 1 arrived, the hotel manager insisted that the All American Girls remain in their rooms. Opposing political factions sometimes fought on May Day, and the manager feared that the players would be unsafe on the streets. "The only way we could get anything to eat," said Annabelle Lee, "was to lower a basket and some money to Cuban boys. They bought us Cokes and pineapples from a stand nearby."

On their way home, the league teams paired up for barnstorming on the East Coast. In one Florida town, some players from California made the mistake of taking seats at the back of a bus. In the segregated South of the late 1940s, buses were divided into front sections for white people and back sections for blacks. "It was uncomfortable, a lot of people stared at us," said Annabelle Lee, "but we wouldn't move."

———— All-Star Stats ————

The 1947 season produced the third perfect game in the league, pitched by Doris Sams for the Muskegon Lassies on August 18 against Fort Wayne. Sams had been an outfielder whose strong overhand throwing arm came into play on the mound, as the league gradually shifted to sidearm in 1946 and 1947 and then to overhand pitching in 1948. (By 1948 the league would insist that all pitchers throw overhand—to give batters a better chance at hitting the ball. Overhand pitchers could not control the ball as well as sidearm or underhand pitchers, and thus allowed more base hits. The result was a livelier game.)

Sams helped her team to the top of the league and was chosen the 1947 Player of the Year for her best won-lost percentage, .733. She also played a full schedule as an outfielder and batted third among the regulars at .280.

A top batting average of .306 was held by Dottie Kamenshek of Rockford, who also boasted the best five-year batting average in the league. Sophie Kurys of Racine again led the league in stolen bases, with 142. This made her five-year total 668—more than halfway to the 1,114 she'd accumulate in all. The major-league record for stolen bases in a single season is 130, attained over 50 more games than the women played. If Kurys had

1947
OFFICIAL
SCHEDULE
South Bend Blue Sox
of the
ALL-AMERICAN GIRLS
BASEBALL LEAGUE
•
PLAYLAND PARK
Home of The Blue Sox
•
Office: LASALLE HOTEL
Phone: 3-3205

All-Star Dottie Kamenshek

maintained her pace over a 162-game season, she would have stolen around 200 bases a year. Comparisons like this don't recognize that the base paths in the women's game were shorter than the 90-foot paths in major league baseball, but they do suggest Kurys' astonishing speed and consistency.

The Color Barrier

Until the late 1940s, black people and white people played in separate baseball leagues. No black women played in the All American Girls League, and no black men played in the major leagues until Jackie Robinson joined the Brooklyn Dodgers in 1947. He was soon followed by Larry Doby with the Cleveland Indians. A year later, the most famous player from the so-called Negro leagues, Satchel Paige, also joined the Indians. In time he was inducted into the Baseball Hall of Fame in Cooperstown, New York. A black woman, Toni Stone (above) from St. Paul, Minnesota, played on a Negro league team, the Indianapolis Clowns, which she joined in 1949.

Joining Sams, Kamenshek, and Kurys on the All-Star team was outfielder Audrey Wagner of Kenosha, who batted just one digit lower than Kamenshek. Wagner led the league in almost every other hitting department, including total hits, extra base hits, doubles, home runs, runs batted in, and total advanced bases. Her extra base blows and two-base hits set league records. Peoria captain Mary Reynolds was selected to play third base with the All-Stars for her "excellent rifle arm and demonstrated power at the plate." She had an outstanding fielding percentage of 1.000, meaning that she played an error-free season.

Other All-Stars for the season included pitcher Millie Earp of Grand Rapids, who rated top billing for her record of 20 wins against eight losses and a league-record earned run average of 0.68. Anna Mae Hutchison of Racine also hurled herself into the All-Stars for a second season. She won the most games in the league, 27, and pitched the most innings, 360, most complete games, 36, and most shutouts, 12. Dottie Mueller from Peoria was the first sidearm pitcher in the All-Stars—winning 21 games, appearing in a record 48, and placing second in innings pitched.

Manufacturers and advertisers attempted to take Rosie the Riveter out of the factory and settle her back into the kitchen.

Banner Years

By 1947 the transformation of league ball from a substitute for the men's game to a sport in its own right was complete. Though more changes in diamond configuration, ball size, and pitching style were still to come, the sport had carved out a niche in the middle of the country, had totaled up its own eye-popping statistics, and had created a group of seasoned players who knew what they could do and wanted to keep doing it.

Life in the United States changed remarkably after the war, and codes of conduct for women became even more strict. As soldiers, sailors, and marines came home and took back their places in factories, service stations, and ballparks, women

Up to the Plate

Postwar advertisements glorified housekeeping and motherhood.

were expected to marry and raise children. Manufacturers and advertisers attempted to take Rosie the Riveter out of the factory and settle her back into the kitchen. Fabrics that had gone into parachutes were now used to make soft, quilted robes for veterans' wives. In *Life* magazine, ads for new cars promised returned soldiers that they could take the driver's seat.

Female ballplayers didn't quite fit into society's new gender stereotypes. But for a while, at least, the All American Girls continued to attract fans with their vigorous playing, eye-catching uniforms, and unusual lifestyles.

The 1947 season brought some surprising victories and upsets. Previous champs, the Racine Belles, took home from Havana the Esther Williams trophy—named after the movie and swimming star of the 1940s—for winning the spring training competitions. Racine started the regular season at the top of the league, but its roster was so small that the team had to play without injury to stay there. Late in the season, two key players were hurt, and the second-year Muskegon Lassies went ahead to clinch the league title.

The Lassies thus went from sixth place in 1946 to first in 1947, with a strong pitching staff, including Annabelle Lee and Doris Sams, excellent defensive skill, and strong all-around hitting. The All American Girls had caught on in a big way in Muskegon, and a record 140,000 fans showed up for the season. The city's Marsh Field held 6,548 fans on Labor Day of 1947. They had come out to watch the league-leading team try to hit home runs over the long fences of this regular, minor-league baseball field.

In the Shaughnessy Playoffs that year, Racine squared off with the Lassies, and the Grand Rapids Chicks went up against the South Bend Blue Sox. The Belles took the first two games and the fourth, disappointing the Lassies' hopes in four games. Anna Mae Hutchinson pitched all three wins for the Belles, the last in relief.

Little Sisters

As local stars, the league players attracted many young fans who wanted to play ball too. During the 1947 season, the league started a number of junior teams for high school girls in the league hometowns. Junior teams held spring tryouts just like the regular teams and used the same rules and equipment as the All American Girls. Juniors also sported uniforms matching their big sisters.

Former baseball and sports stars from each town coached and umpired for the junior teams. The girls' teams were financed by the parent clubs, and, in some instances, the juniors played on league fields just before the All American Girls took over. Some towns even extended the junior season into championship playoffs, and fans were given the chance to vote for most valuable or impressive players.

In Racine, Nancy Anderson was awarded a 1947 Junior Player of the Year trophy from the Belles and won a trip to the league's 1948 spring tryouts. Thus, the junior girls teams helped develop future league players, experienced in the All American Girls' special brand of baseball.

The Chicks and the Blue Sox fought for five games, with Grand Rapids punching out five runs in the eighth inning of the fifth game to win 6-1. The Chicks also played error-free ball against the many errors of South Bend. But South Bend catcher Bonnie Baker led the hitters of the series with .389 and "literally stole the fourth game for her team with a daring theft of home and the only run that scored."

The final series that year went for seven rather than five games. This time, the traditional rivals from Racine and Grand Rapids took each other on, but it didn't rain buckets, and the umpire kept his eye on the play. The Chicks had also acquired a new manager, Johnny Rawlings, a major league veteran and a World Series hero from the early 1920s.

The first three games went into extra innings, and Belle Anna Mae Hutchinson appeared in all three, winning the first. The second, third, and fourth games went to the Chicks, with Chicks hurler Millie Earp showing exceptional strength in the fourth and looking to wrap up the series. But the Belles, led by Hutchinson, pulled a surprise

Manager Johnny Rawlings talks strategy with the Chicks.

victory in the fifth game, making the series total three games for the Chicks and two for the Belles. The sixth game was played to a 3-3 tie in the last half of the ninth inning, when a push from the Belles put them over for a one-run victory.

Finally, in the seventh game, with Racine catcher Irene Hickson playing with a broken finger, each team played its best pitcher, Hutchinson (Belles) for her eighth appearance in 11 playoff games, and Earp for the Chicks. Fans predicted that the stingy pitchers would keep a tight rein on the hits. They were right. By the seventh inning, with no score and practically no activity from batters on either side, Hutchinson gave up a base on balls, and the Chicks finally scored off the walk to end the breathtaking suspense. It was the first championship for the Chicks, whose infield played excellent defensive ball, with the keystone combination of shortstop Ernestine Petras and second sacker Alma Ziegler cutting short many scoring attempts. Connie Wisniewski not only pitched well but also led all batters of the two final teams.

Annabelle Lee remembered that the team made some money and that each player got a ring with the word "Chicks" written in the shape of a heart. Each also received a gold pen decorated with crossed bats and a baseball. "I felt lucky to be a winner," she said. It was the end of her league career. Late in the season, she had hurt herself sliding into home, had become partially paralyzed, and had returned to California to recover.

In 1948 the league firmly adopted the overhand pitching style, encouraging sidearm or underarm players to switch. The switch discouraged some veterans, who retired from the league. Others, like Connie Wisniewski, decided to give up pitching for positions in the outfield and to work on their hitting. Still others, like Dottie Wiltse Collins, learned the new style. "I could pitch both ways," she said, "but my curve ball was better underhand than overhand."

The new season brought other changes, as the league fine-tuned its game. Along with the new

Underhand pitching disappeared in 1948.

pitching style, the ball again decreased in size, from 11 to 10⅜ inches around. Base paths were extended from 70 to 72 feet, and the pitching distance grew from 43 feet to 50. The All American Girls were playing a game that more and more resembled standard baseball.

Two new clubs were added to the league in 1948, making a total of ten. The Chicago Colleens, managed by Dave Bancroft (formerly of the New York Giants), were slated to play on Chicago's southwest side. In Springfield, Illinois, the second new team, the Sallies, would be managed by Carson Bigbee, a former Pittsburgh Pirates outfielder and star of the 1925 World Series.

After spring training in a deserted air force base at Opa-Locka, Florida, the teams were stocked with rookies and veterans from 27 states, Canada, and Cuba. The league was split into two divisions, with Racine, Kenosha, Rockford, Peoria, and Springfield in the western section and Muskegon, Grand Rapids, South Bend, Fort Wayne, and Chicago in the east. Each team would make two complete

The Chicago Colleens

swings through the circuit, thus increasing the number of regular games in the season to 126. Add on two preliminary playoff series, with the top four teams from each section, and a final series with the two section winners, and the league faced an extended season of 144 games. No wonder the players often prayed for rain to give them a break from their heavy, eight-game-a-week schedule.

After a month of play, the Springfield Sallies lost their hometown support and, like the Millerettes, became a traveling team at league expense. But most other teams were enjoying banner years. Fans entering the stadium at Playland in South Bend were greeted by owner Pete Redden, dressed in a straw hat, spats, and a cane, shouting like a carnival barker. Warm-ups before games brought the players out for "pepper ball," where one player pitched, a batter hit to a third player, she pitched to another batter, and so on down a double line. Once games started, hitters had a hard time in the field. The fences were too far back to hit over easily, and outfielders played heavy hitters deep. Most fans didn't care. Some sat in the same spot every night, heckling players who were lagging, cheering those having a good game.

Teenage bat-girl Janet "Peewee" Wiley had a great time at Playland, kidding with an umpire named Barney, who complained that her pitches stung his hand. Blue Sox manager Chet Grant even let her pitch to a few batters once, in a game with Grand Rapids. South Bend rookie Lou Arnold was flattered when young fans asked for her autograph. One five-year-old girl gave Lou a choker, a bracelet, and a picture of herself standing in a tree trunk. The girl's parents brought her to the ball games many nights in a row. Women of all ages liked watching the All American Girls play. They brought their husbands, fathers, uncles, and sons to the ballparks.

Despite the rules about ladylike behavior, the All American Girls were not very prim and proper on the field. Blue Sox catcher Bonnie Baker kicked dust in one umpire's eyes, and Ruth Lessing from

Good ball-playing, which had long been buried behind the camouflage of charm and femininity, was finally getting national attention.

Grand Rapids was thrown out and fined for using unmannerly language to another. Faye Dancer did back flips in center field and sometimes climbed into the stands to conduct seances or display one of the glass animal eyes she collected for good luck. Fans cheered and hooted, and players yelled back at them.

Attendance soared in 1948. Third-year club Peoria upped its count, drawing almost 130,000 for the regular season. Grand Rapids upheld a previous top-notch position with 150,000; Rockford rebounded with 130,000. Small Kenosha enjoyed its best attendance in six years, and the other established clubs drew nearly 100,000. By the end of the season, including the extended playoffs, the All American Girls had dazzled close to a million fans.

When the 1948 season was over, the eastern section winner was the Grand Rapids Chicks; the western section was taken by the Racine Belles. The Player of the Year was the top hitter for the season, Audrey Wagner from the Kenosha Comets. Her batting average was .312, seven points higher than the year before.

It was a year of many no-hit, no-run games, with 16 pitched in all. Despite changes to liven up the ball and make the hits go farther, the game was still dominated by pitching. Even the change to

1948 Player of the Year Audrey Wagner (far right) shares reading material with some Kenosha teammates.

overhand did not take the oomph out of balls that pitchers put across the plate.

By now 21 players had been with the league for six years, and 34 for five years. In a group of around 170 players, this skilled and savvy third no doubt was a major reason for the league's outstanding success in 1948. When the championship dust had settled, it lay on the mantel of the Rockford Peaches, who had come from behind to whip the top-seeded Chicks and Belles.

For some players, the excitement didn't stop on the ball field. Red Wing Faye Dancer had a gangster boyfriend, who followed her from town to town in a bulletproof blue Packard. In 1948, when her parents came from California to see her play, she rewarded them by hitting two doubles and a single. At the party afterward, champagne flowed, and the gangster promised Faye a golden palomino and her parents a new car if she would stay in Peoria.

Another boyfriend, a judge, gave Faye a diamond engagement ring. "Why the heck are you giving me a ring?" she asked. She had the diamond taken out and she put it in her baseball ring. It was clear where her heart belonged.

Isabel Alvares was one of many young players assigned to the Colleens.

5

Bases Loaded, Bottom of the Ninth

Could the league keep up its success of 1948? Several things dimmed its prospects. The two new teams, the Chicago Colleens and the Springfield Sallies, were filled with many new players and did not catch on in their hometowns. The Sallies became a traveling team early in the 1948 season. By 1949 both new teams had taken to the road.

Neither competed with the regular league teams, but instead barnstormed throughout various regions, playing each other and making women's baseball a more and more common sight. They also served as farm teams for the established league teams. New recruits, especially younger women not yet out of their teens, often spent a season or two traveling with the Sallies or the Colleens.

In whirlwind style, the two teams traveled together, entered a town, had tryouts for new players, played a game, and sometimes left the same day. "I left so many things behind, dragging my bags," Isabel Alvares remembers. She was assigned to the Colleens in 1949.

Peewee Wiley, former bat-girl for South Bend, also joined the Colleens. She was 17. When they traveled on the bus, she and "Lefty" Alvares would read to each other from comic books to help Lefty improve her English. The teams stopped in Lynchburg and Bluefield, Virginia, and got as far as Macon, Georgia, when Blue Sox manager Karl Winsch decided that he wanted Peewee to join the South Bend team as a regular. Sent alone by plane to South Bend, she recalled, "I was a scared 17-year-old on a little plane, bumping its way over mountains. If I'd stayed with the Colleens, I'd have had a chance to play in Yankee Stadium and meet Mickey Mantle." The Yankees' star was only a year older than Peewee.

Trying to capitalize on their veterans but also provide training for rookies, many teams observed a "rookie rule." They added rookies only as fielders. When it came time to hit, more practiced players stood in the lineup. Thus teams increased from 15 to around 18 players.

Salaries for young rookies were low: Peewee made $25 a week in her first year. Lou Arnold started at $65 a week in 1948, but she was 10 years older and more experienced. Veterans like Betsy Jochum and Lib Mahon from South Bend made up to $100 a week, which was, they thought, the tops. Then they learned that fiery Bonnie Baker, an outstanding catcher and popular hitter, made quite a bit more. It was rumored that her salary was $200 or even $300 a week.

Shortstop Dottie Shroeder played with the league for all 12 seasons.

Will the League Last?

By 1949 hometown support for the league teams had begun to fall off a little, and veterans were starting to leave. Faye Dancer retired after the 1950 season in Peoria, remarking, "I've always said when something I love begins to decline, it's time to leave."

But Fort Wayne's Dottie Wiltse Collins, pregnant with her first child, kept right on pitching. In that era, pregnancy was usually a signal to send a woman home from the job, whether she felt fine or not. No one suggested that it was unwomanly or dangerous for Dottie, though. Her doctor encouraged her to keep exercising, and she pitched into her sixth month. She took a year off and returned for one more season in 1950. "I made a great comeback," she reported, "then I said, that's it!"

Staffed by inexperienced rookies, the Racine Belles lost five of their first seven games in 1950. The Racine *Journal Times* kidded Belles manager Norman "Nummy" Derringer about losing his temper with the team: Was he ready to "chuck a few of his players off the roof?" Derringer explained that the Belles would have won if he'd used veteran players. But the only way "to develop rookies is to play them—and the place to play them is in spring games," he said.

Don Black was now the Belles' president and a member of the league Balancing Committee. He negotiated some trades to balance the weaker rookie players. But by the end of the season, the Belles had not played up to their former standings, and the city leaders decided not to renew their sponsorship. Attendance at Muskegon had also declined enough to discourage the hometown directors. Racine and Muskegon withdrew from the league after the 1950 season.

These exits may also have been caused by a change in the organization as a whole. Arthur Meyerhoff, the lawyer who had taken over the league's management from Philip K. Wrigley, stepped down in 1950. With this, the league lost some of its central direction. Civic leaders were still willing to finance the shortfalls that teams usually accumulated each year, and they still collaborated on publicity, rules, and scheduling. But promotion for the whole league was not the same. The strong management of Wrigley, then Meyerhoff, had contributed substantially to making the All American Girls a household name in the Midwest.

Yet the women's teams were still thriving. Attendance in the 1950 season was again close to a

Lib Mahon

Kenosha sluggers: Phyllis Koehn, Lou Colacite, and Jerry O'Hara

million, and national magazines featured upbeat articles about the All American Girls. When Racine and Muskegon pulled out, two Michigan towns immediately took up the franchises—the Belles moved to Battle Creek and the Lassies went to Kalamazoo.

In 1951 *McCall's* magazine sent writer Morris Markey to size up the All American Girls. He was surprised at the "10,000 yells in the grandstand" as two runs came in. The league was "more than a sporting enterprise," he insisted. It was a singular chance for "deft and determined girls—thousands of them, in the potential—to harvest a warming spot in the limelight, plus a very handy bank account."

Markey didn't hesitate to discuss the female side of the players' lives. "Hey, Mom, You're Out," was the title of his article, and he featured the mothers in the league, notably Blue Sox pitcher Jean Faut in a full-page photograph with her husband, Blue Sox manager Karl Winsch, and two-year-old son.

But Markey also played up the league in an unusual way for the period. He delighted in the players' skill and competitiveness as athletes rather than "ladies," and he emphasized how rarely women can compete in sports as equals or superiors to men.

From Player to Manager

Bonnie Baker was the only player and the only woman ever to manage an All American Girls team. A catcher with the South Bend Blue Sox, Baker was a favorite with the fans. "She always had time to talk to youngsters and autograph a program," remembers her teammate Ruth Williams.

The Kalamazoo Lassies had a bad year when they first moved from Muskegon in 1949, ending the season in last place. So in 1950 the league fired the Lassies' manager and brought in Bonnie Baker to replace him. She immediately began to build the team, trading for some of her old teammates from South Bend. Williams remembered Baker as "no nonsense on the field .... she was hard as nails ... and was appalled that some Kalamazoo players knew so little about the intricacies of the game."

The Lassies played hard for Baker, and they began to climb out of the cellar. By the end of the 1950 season, Baker had led her team to fourth place. The older, male managers were supposed to be more knowledgeable from years of major- and minor-league play. But, as Williams explained, "[Baker] understood women better than they did."

The fans picked up on the intensity of the play and, curious to see the first female manager, flocked to the ballpark. "Baker did a lot to sell the game to the fans," said Williams. "She did radio shows, appeared at grocery store promotions dressed to the nines. People wanted to be around her." After the 1950 season, Baker took a year off to have a baby. She returned to the Lassies in 1952 and played as catcher for one more season.

The 1949 Blue Sox with Bonnie Baker (back row, far left)

Up to the Plate

Jean Faut was one of
several ball-playing
mothers.

Playing "all out" and having the "opportunity to show that you are good at something, to have people yell their approval of you, injects powerful ingredients into the soul," he concluded. Almost too late, good ball-playing, which had been buried for too long behind the camouflage of charm and femininity, was getting national attention.

——— Here Come The Blue Sox ———

When spring training opened at Playland in 1951, Blue Sox manager Karl Winsch found ways to trim his team down from 32 hopefuls to 25. (Trying to build up their roster of future full-timers, many teams had added a number of rookies who did not play through each game.) Some excellent players remained with the team. Pitcher Jean Faut, who led the season in 1950 with 21 wins, 9 losses, and an ERA of 1.12, was backed up by Lou Arnold, Sue Kidd, Lil Faralla, and Jerry Vincent.

The Blue Sox began strong, with Lib Mahon's two-base hit driving in a run to win the season opener 1-0. In another early game, Mahon slapped out the season's first homer, Dottie Mueller came in from first base to take up pitching again, and she hurled the Sox to a 4-1 win over Kenosha. The Blue Sox swept six victories, and by the end of the season's first half, they held third place under the Grand Rapids Chicks and the Fort Wayne Daisies.

Starting the second half of the season, Jean Faut pitched a perfect game against Rockford, the fourth in league history. The local paper reported: "The chances of a perfect game were never mentioned in the Blue Sox dugout during the game, according to baseball superstition, but the crowd of 1490 were fully aware that baseball history was in the making."

Shortly afterward, Lou Arnold pitched a shutout against Battle Creek, with the Sox winning 7-0. Lou's wintertime employer in Rhode Island had stopped in to see her pitch, and he commented to the Pawtucket, Rhode Island, newspaper: "Believe me, it's something. Those girls play real ball. It's fast, colorful, and real interesting. It was all a big surprise to me."

Now the Blue Sox were on a roll, nine wins in a row, with a three-game lead in the second half of the season. When the decisive game against Rockford was played, on September 2, 1951, the Blue Sox defeated their rival 5-1, with strong pitching by

Lou Arnold, 1951

Sox Sue Kidd. During the championship playoffs, South Bend and Fort Wayne each took a game before the Blue Sox squeezed a second win in the tenth inning of game three.

In the final series, South Bend and Rockford were at it again. Rockford won the first two games. "Same Old Story!" announced the newspaper, "Jean Faut to Hurl Critical Game for South Bend Sox." In the third game, Faut was nicked early for single runs, both scored by Dottie Kamenshek. Then, in the third inning, Faut hit a double and teammates helped to bring in three Blue Sox runs. That's where the scoring stayed for the rest of the game. Faut heated up her fastball, but Peaches rookie Marie Mansfield threw lots of wild pitches. In the fourth game, the Blue Sox evened up the series by keeping the batting pressure on two Rockford pitching veterans, Rose Gacioch and Helen Nicol Fox.

In the final game, before "2268 exuberant fans at Playland," the Blue Sox clinched the 1951 championship 10-2, supporting pitchers Lil Faralla and Jean Faut with a 13-hit attack. In the first inning, the Sox scored five runs. They added single runs in the second, third, and fourth innings, and a two-run cluster in the eighth. South Bend had finally brought home a championship, and fans streamed onto the field to carry the winning team off on their shoulders.

Faut pitched South Bend to victory in 1951.

Big Hitters

Two more teams dropped from sight after the 1951 season: the Kenosha Comets and the Peoria Red Wings. The smallest city in the league, Kenosha had struggled more than the larger towns to absorb yearly deficits and to keep up its financial commitments to the players. Kenosha and the Battle Creek Belles had both almost withdrawn from the league in the middle of the 1951 season, but local businesses had propped up the Belles, and Kenosha had limped along until the end of the season—with talk of the team going to Dubuque, Iowa. Attendance declined the last two years for the Red Wings, making the decision to fold the team easier. For the 1952 season, the league would play with six teams.

In the remaining towns—South Bend, Rockford, Kalamazoo, Fort Wayne, Battle Creek, and Grand Rapids, the All American Girls were playing as competitive and dramatic a game as ever. Play was even more lively, with more hitting and more home runs. The fences at Playland, much too long for consistent home-run hitting, had been brought in to 225 feet at right and left field. The smaller, livelier ball, closer fences, and greater distances in the diamond helped give the advantage to batters, with teams totaling 11, 15, and even 24 runs per game.

But there simply weren't as many fans as before. Five years earlier, the attendance for a championship game would have been triple the numbers that came out to see the Blue Sox take their first banner in league history. What caused the change?

Grand Rapids Chicks Betty Wickam, Twy Shively, Joyce Hill, Marge Wenzel, and Philomina Giafrancisco

Up to the Plate

By the early 1950s, almost all remnants of the hardships of World War II had been erased in the United States. With a prosperous economy, many Americans didn't need hometown sports for cheap entertainment anymore. With cars more plentiful, families began to move to the suburbs, leaving behind the city centers where many ball fields were located. They drove out of town on weekends to lake cabins and resorts. Young people gathered at drive-in movies and restaurants. And TVs appeared in the living rooms of many homes—people could now watch major-league baseball on television.

Dottie Ferguson, Rockford Peaches

The country no longer knew what to make of the All American Girls either. A Movietone newsreel about the Kalamazoo Lassies gave a confusing portrayal of team members as swimsuit queens and kitchen hostesses, as well as sliding, scrappy, hard-hitting ballplayers. Roles for women had become more and more rigid, and fewer people were curious enough to give young women a chance to show how well they could play ball.

But the All American Girls had a few good years left. Nancy Mudge, a graduate of Taylor University in Indiana, began as a second sacker with the Colleens in the summer of 1950. She played a while before being injured, and in 1951 signed on as a regular for the Kalamazoo Lassies. "To do what we did and get paid for it was like a dream," she said, and "we didn't throw like girls."

Indeed, league players disproved the myth that women can't throw a baseball well. They knew how to bring the throwing arm back, shift their weight to the opposite foot, and uncoil for power and accuracy. By this time, the league had dropped the ball size below 10 inches and had extended the base paths to 80 feet and the mound-to-home plate distance to 57. Players needed all the oomph they could get to send the ball over these longer paths.

By now, the league was dominated by the Fort Wayne Daisies. Jimmie Foxx—one of baseball's greatest sluggers with 58 home runs for the 1932 Philadelphia Athletics—became the new manager of the Daisies in 1952.

The Daisies got off to a good start that season, winning the opening game 8-1 over the Lassies. A number of players showed their stuff in the game: 18-year-old pitcher Maxine Kline hurled to only 32 players and held the Lassies to one run. A bevy of hitting sisters, Betty (Weaver) Foss and Jean and Jo Weaver, slammed hits right and left, getting 4 of the total 13.

Meanwhile, the Daisies were trading for good players, announcing that Pepper Paire would return to the team after a seven-year absence. They also picked up 17-year-old Jean Havlish, who took the

One wealthy Fort Wayne backer canceled his Chicago Cubs tickets and bought a season ticket for the All American Girls.

train by herself from St. Paul, Minnesota, to Fort Wayne to try out for the team.

Taking on the 1951 champs, the Daisies beat the South Bend Blue Sox 1-0 in 12 innings. Maxine Kline earned her fifth straight victory, with excellent fielding support of only one error, and retired the "formidable Jean Faut." It was the Daisies' seventh win in nine games; they were one game out of first place. Finally, at the end of the season, the Daisies topped the league for the first time.

Each Daisy received a watch, a bonus check, and a white sweater identifying the team as league leaders. "Manager Jimmie Foxx...was deeply moved when the players presented him with a handsome trophy," reported the local paper. "He thought the trophy should go into his niche in baseball's Hall of Fame." Next the Daisies won the first round of the Shaughnessy Playoffs against Rockford, with excellent hitting, including many doubles by the Weaver sisters, a double steal by Ruth Richard, and Maxine Kline's feisty pitching.

Preparing to meet Fort Wayne in the finals, the Blue Sox were handicapped by the loss of six valuable players. A rebellion had started when manager Karl Winsch suspended second baser Shorty Pryer for taking off her shoes on the field. Five other players walked off in protest, and the manager promptly added their names to the list of suspensions. South Bend played the final series with a roster of only 12 players. But even with this handicap, the Blue Sox won the series, their second playoff championship in a row.

By 1953 Jean Havlish had secured a solid place in the Daisies' lineup. Bill Allington, who had coached the Rockford Peaches for years, came in to replace Jimmie Foxx. The league had lost the Battle Creek Belles at the end of 1952, and a number of veterans were retiring. Allington fashioned an all-rookie infield for the opening game, with Jean Havlish as the shortstop.

The Daisies were playing well in 1953, with two of the Weaver sisters, Betty Foss and Jo Weaver, leading the league in batting—Jo with .371 and

Bill Allington

Betty with .347. Batting averages as a whole had jumped higher when the smaller, livelier ball became the standard. In the smallest field, in Kalamazoo, a larger ball was used to cut down on home runs.

The Daisies won an All-Star exhibition game against South Bend, but the Blue Sox led in the league standings with a nine-game winning streak. By August, a newly formed league team named the Muskegon Belles had lost their home ground and been sent out on the road as orphans. Nancy Mudge, who'd been traded from Kalamazoo to help start the Belles, was having a good hitting year, racking up three runs off one hit in a win against the Daisies. By the end of August, the Daisies led the league by a seven-game margin, but attendance was sagging at 5,000 less than the year before. The Rockford Peaches were also having a rough time, and they ran an ad asking for civic donations to keep the club going.

Meanwhile, the wandering Muskegon Belles captured a shutout victory, 6-0, against the Daisies on August 28. The Daisies did produce one spectacular triple play in the seventh inning, the first of the year for the entire league. But by the end of the season, the upset was a thing of the past, and the Daisies had emerged at the head of the league. In the playoffs, the Grand Rapids Chicks came from behind for a surprising victory. But that didn't bother one wealthy Fort Wayne backer, who was so enthusiastic about the Daisies that he canceled his Chicago Cubs tickets and bought a season ticket for the All American Girls.

When the 1954 season started, there was talk about changing the ball size and diamond dimensions again. If the American public wanted to watch baseball, maybe the All American Girls should give them exactly that. Finally, in July, the league adopted the standard nine-inch baseball, moved the base paths to 85 feet (baseball's are 90), and expanded the plate-to-mound distance to 60 feet (baseball's is 60½).

For the first time in her career, Jean Havlish

June Peppas of the Kalamazoo Lassies, 1953

became something of a hitter. It was a Daisies' tradition that when a player hit a whopping good game, she went downtown to a local sporting goods store and picked out a new bat. With batting averages of .190 and .240, Havlish rarely had a chance to do that. But in one game during the 1954 season, she went four for four. Proud to be in the company of big hitters, she went downtown and charged a new bat to the club. The store notified the paper, and Jean's picture made the next day's news.

She also gave Bill Allington the ammunition he needed to settle a decision. Now that the game was more or less like regulation baseball, should the Daisies push back their fences to match standard fields? One night Jean hit two home runs. "That does it," said Allington, as Jean came home the second time. "When Havlish hits home runs, we move the fences back." The next day the players faced a bigger field, and Jean hit no more home runs.

Despite these changes and the resulting lively ball games, the league was floundering. It was

The Lassies were a top team in 1954, and many Lassies made the All-Star squad (below).

harder and harder to find seasoned players. As one catcher commented, the women played every bit as well in the field and on the mound as their male counterparts, but they didn't hit with as much accuracy. Perhaps if they had had the same years of training in minor leagues as did most male players, the All American Girls could have made up for that deficiency. But no minor-league system existed for the women. And hometown backers were not making enough in ticket sales to pay the players their weekly wages. Catcher Joyce Hill Westerman quit the league after an eight-year career, because there was "hesitation about getting our checks, and the teams weren't drawing good crowds anymore."

But for newcomers who never expected to be playing professional ball "under the lights," and for veterans like Lassie Dottie Schroeder, turning in their gloves had no appeal. In 1954 Schroeder could still get in a bang-up argument with an umpire. After colliding with the Daisy's Jean Geissinger, Schroeder took on the umpire for waving Geissinger on to the next base. "The whole Kalamazoo team got in the argument," reported the local paper, "but it didn't matter because Geissinger didn't score." Maybe in the short term, it didn't matter. But these were the Shaughnessy Playoffs, and the Lassies were fighting to even up the series and get a first-time shot at the championship. The game ended with the Lassies winning 2-1 in 10 innings.

The Lassies were a Cinderella team—a long shot to win—in more ways than one. Not only had Fort Wayne taken the league season victory for the third straight year, but just before going into the series, the Lassies had lost two pitchers. One's mother had died and she'd gone home. The other had shut her hand in a car door. When the team was given the option to play shorthanded or pick up a pitcher, they voted to play as they were. "Pride, I guess," explained Nancy Mudge.

She remembered the last out of the seventh, tie-breaking game with Fort Wayne. A ground ball came to her at second base. "I looked over to first

Men's baseball effectively closed its doors to women in 1952.

base and saw Jeanie Lovell down on her knees, ready to receive it for the out. She was not going to miss that ball." She didn't, and the Kalamazoo Lassies won the 1954 championship.

———————— *The End of an Era* ————————

The following winter, Jean Havlish received a letter saying that the league had folded. She was devastated. The glorious excitement and hard playing of her league days were over after only two full seasons. She wanted the league to continue, and a lot of other players felt the same way. Bill Allington put together a traveling team to barnstorm for the summer of 1955, but it did not last. The All American Girls Professional Baseball League had become a casualty of the country's peacetime prosperity.

After the league folded, there was little or no opportunity for women to play baseball other than in amateur leagues. Men's baseball had closed its doors effectively to women in 1952, when a shortstop named Eleanor Engle almost signed with the minor-league Harrisburg Senators in the Inter-State League. To keep her from playing, National League Association president George Trautman prohibited female players, and major-league commissioner Ford Frick voided Engle's contract. On June 23, 1952, Frick banned women from the minor leagues.

Now that the All American Girls Baseball League had folded, most of the players turned to softball or other sports like golf and bowling. A number became physical education teachers in high schools and colleges and coached various women's sports programs. They kept in touch with the close friends they had made as All American Girls, but they didn't talk about the league to strangers.

"I didn't tell people for years that I played baseball," commented Kay Heim McDaniel. "They wouldn't have believed me. They'd have called for the straitjacket and hauled me off to the loony bin." Thirty years would pass before the women would contact each other and begin to reflect on the

> *"If women were given the same opportunities as men, they would definitely be playing ball."*

unusual experiences that they had shared on the ball field.

Millerettes, 1944

——— The League Lives On ———

For nearly 30 years, the story of the league fell silent. Opportunities narrowed for American women during the 1950s and early 1960s. Denied access to many jobs and sports programs, women lost the chance to show that they could be skilled athletes and professionals. Then, in the late 1960s and early 1970s, modern feminists began to protest artificial limits and false stereotypes imposed on women. They set the stage for the league's story to be revived and to receive the attention and respect it deserved.

Finally, in 1982, a group of former league players founded the All American Girls Players' Association. More and more former players came forward, and the association began to hold huge reunions. These meetings, and a newsletter that went to every member, helped players collect the physical remains and memories of the league: news clippings and yearbooks, bats and gloves, uniforms and balls—in six sizes.

The league players were finally able to convince a skeptical public that they deserved a place in ball-playing history. In 1988 the Baseball Hall of Fame in Cooperstown, New York, created a permanent exhibit honoring the All American Girls. When they gathered to view the display case, with the different-sized balls, a uniform, gloves, and wonderful photos, many players finally felt rewarded for their playing. A number of Canadian provinces also honored their ballplayers with exhibits and ceremonies. Several documentaries brought scenes of the league, both past and present, to TV screens. People enjoyed seeing the former players, now in their fifties and sixties, still pitching, hitting, and running.

The Hall of Fame in Cooperstown honors women in baseball with a special display.

Bases Loaded, Bottom of the Ninth

A League of Their Own, *with stars Lori Petty and Geena Davis, helped renew interest in the league.*

Then, in 1992, director Penny Marshall's movie *A League of Their Own* told a fictionalized league story to eager summertime audiences. The movie was a hit. Tom Hanks played a hard-drinking, washed-up major leaguer who manages an All American Girls team. Geena Davis and Lori Petty were baseball-playing sisters, one a catcher, the other a pitcher. Madonna played a flirtatious, gum-snapping crowd pleaser, and Rosie O'Donnell was a rough-and-ready player with a mouth to match. Not only was the film good entertainment, but it also helped educate the public about women's athletics. Parents of girls who said they wanted to be catchers and pitchers began to pay attention. Maybe professional ball-playing for young women wasn't such a silly idea.

Though they were thrilled about the movie, some league players complained a bit. Tom Hanks as the drunken manager wasn't anything like managers they remember—kindly gentlemen who never entered the women's locker rooms and never appeared drunk on the field. Leaguers also complained that the movie stars who played their younger selves—Madonna, Geena Davis, and Rosie O'Donnell—threw "a lot like girls." But on the whole, former players agreed that the movie was a glorious tribute.

The last scenes of the movie show actresses and some real league players attending the opening of the Baseball Hall of Fame exhibit, then playing an exhibition game on the diamond at Cooperstown. These heroes of the league, now grandmothers and senior citizens, can still hit the stuffing out of a baseball. As the movie drew public attention to the league, many players were honored by their own hometowns. Kay Heim McDaniel and Nancy Mudge Cato tossed out the first balls at a Minnesota Twins baseball game. "I was worried I'd forgotten how to throw," said McDaniel. "But I got out there on the mound and wound up and felt as if the years since the league didn't exist at all. The ball went right over the plate."

Today, league players sign baseballs and mitts for young girls who want to be ballplayers themselves. The girls might see their dreams come true. In 1994, a new women's baseball team, the Colorado Silver Bullets, entered the minor leagues. The Bullets are managed by former major-league pitcher Phil Niekro. "I think it's time," he said. "The world wants to know if females can play against men."

More than one thousand women tried out for the 45 invitations to spring training in Orlando, Florida. Teachers, writers, landscape designers, bookkeepers, nannies, waitresses, social workers, private investigators—all kinds of women wanted to make the team. Gina Satriano, a Los Angeles County assistant district attorney, said: "If women were given the same opportunities as men, they would definitely be playing ball." A pitcher, her throws clocked at 80 miles per hour, Satriano "can't believe the change is here...we're going to run into a lot of adversity, but what I'm hoping this does is change some minds."

Bases Loaded, Bottom of the Ninth

Silver Bullet pitcher Charlotte Wiley warms up.

Originally planning to play against men's minor-league teams, the Silver Bullets were trounced in early games and changed their strategy. Their new opponents would be men's amateur teams made up of players aged 35 and older.

The Bullets first win, over the Richfield (Minnesota) Rockets, came seven games into the season. Rallying from a 2–0 lag, the Bullets scored seven runs in the sixth and seventh innings to send a sell-out crowd to its feet. Bullets pitcher Lee Anne Ketcham struck out 14 batters in the victory. All American Girls veterans Jean Havlish, Kay Heim McDaniel, and Nancy Mudge Cato each threw out a pitch to open the game.

The All American Girls Players' Association would like to see a revival of an all-women's league as well. When this happens, the young women who are called up to the pros will know whom to thank. Their foremothers from the All American Girls Professional Baseball League will cheer them on for their seasons under the lights.

Author's Acknowledgments

We are lucky that so many women who played in the All American Girls Professional Baseball League are still alive. Three of them, living near me around the Twin Cities of Minneapolis–St. Paul, have proved not only valuable sources of information and stories, but good friends as well. Thank you, Kay Heim McDaniel, Jean Havlish, and Nancy Mudge Cato. You have helped bring the league to life for me.

Anyone writing about the league these days could not proceed without Dottie Wiltse Collins' friendly, expert knowledge of players, league history, and the players' association. My husband Fran and I spent an enjoyable summer afternoon with Dottie and her husband, Harvey, in Fort Wayne. Thank you, Dottie, for numerous phone conversations, a leaguer's tour of Fort Wayne and your scrapbooks. I have also benefitted from the archives at the National Baseball Hall of Fame and Museum in Cooperstown, New York, and from the league archives at the Northern Indiana Historical Society in South Bend. Thank you, especially Diane Barts and staff in South Bend. A handful of others wrote about the league before me. Thank you particularly to Sharon L. Roepke, whose summary of the league was one of the earliest, notably from a feminist point of view. Finally, for amazingly fresh memories, helpful analysis, and willing conversation, I thank the following players: Faye Dancer for ribald humor and hilarious stories; Annabelle Lee Harmon for careful, detailed reminiscences; Sophie Kurys for lengthy and fascinating personal tales of the league; Joyce Hill Westerman for a pleasant visit, the loan of photographs, yearbooks, and a look at the real thing in league uniforms, balls, and mitts; Lou Arnold, Betsy Jochum, Lib Mahon, and Janet (Peewee) Wiley Sears—the South Bend contingent—for lively and enjoyable meetings; and again Lou Arnold for mailing a scrapbook, an act far beyond the call of duty.

Thanks continued to Isabel Alvares for an interesting Cuban perspective on the league; to Dottie Key for tracking me down when we both were out of town; to Audrey Kissel Lafser for helpful follow-up on queries; to Karen Kunkel for a description of the players' association's involvement with Penny Marshall's movie; to Irene Applegren and Jo Lenard for personal tales and last-minute confirmation of facts; to Joanne Winter for contacting Ken Sells and helping me puzzle out the meaning of "Shaughnessy," as in playoffs; to Bonnie Baker and Ruth Williams for fascinating details about Baker's stint as the only female league manager; to Beth Johnson and Millie Gerdom, league fans par excellence; to Leo Schrall for good information on his management experience in the league; to Emil Petrangeli for sending an interview about his days as a league umpire; and to Les Allsup for providing a groundskeeper's perspective.

This book would not have come to be without the initial encouragement of editor Leonard Witt of *Minnesota Monthly,* in which I published a short article on the Minneapolis Millerettes, and the encouraging people at Lerner.

V is for Victory

Index

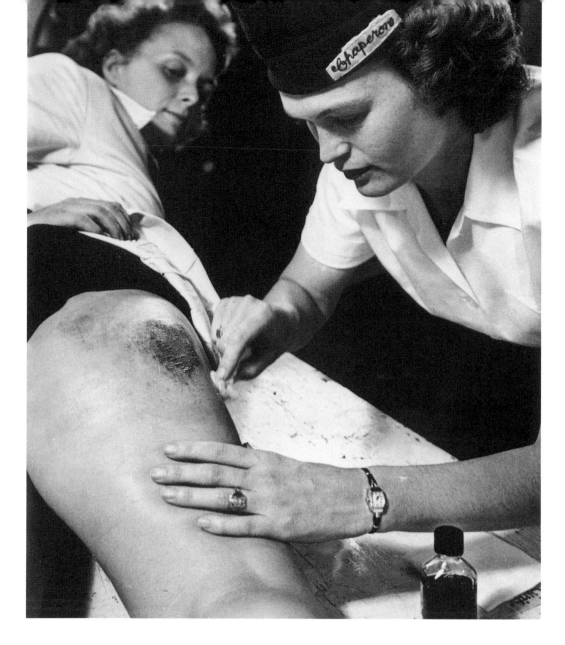

Picture Credits

Photographs and illustrations used with permission of the Northern Indiana Historical Society: pp. 2, 6, 18, 20, 24, 26 (both), 27, 28, 29, 33, 36, 38, 42, 47, 48, 50, 58, 59 (bottom), 64, 65, 66, 70, 72, 73, 75, 77, 78, 82, 83, 87, 88, 96; National Archives: pp. 8, 9, 11 (left), 45; UPI/Bettmann: p. 10; William Wrigley Jr. Company: p. 11 (right); Dottie Wiltse Collins: pp. 13, 31, 32, 44; Kay Heim McDaniel: pp. 14, 22, 23, 52 (right), 68, 74; Faye Dancer: pp. 17, 34, 69; National Baseball Library and Archive, Cooperstown, New York: pp. 25, 40, 51, 53, 57, 76, 80, 93; Joyce Hill Westerman: pp. 39, 46, 49, 54, 56 (both), 79; Margot Galt: pp. 52 (left), 59 (top); Urban Archives, Temple University, Philadelphia: p. 60; The Hoover Company, North Canton, Ohio: p. 62; Nancy Mudge Cato: p. 84; Hollywood Book and Poster: p. 89; John Doman, St. Paul Pioneer Press: p. 91.

Cover photographs: Northern Indiana Historical Society. Author photo by Tim Francisco.